English for Global Communication

Myeong-Hee Seong

Tourist Information & Creative Thinking for Language Learners

지식인

Profile

Myeong-Hee Seong
Ph.D. in English Education, Korea University
Professor, Eulji University

English for Global Communication

Tourist Information & Creative Thinking for Language Learners

2019년 8월 15일 초판 1쇄 인쇄
2019년 8월 20일 초판 1쇄 발행

지은이 | Myeong-Hee Seong
펴낸이 | 김종욱 · 명사동
펴낸곳 | 지식인
등 록 | 제301-2013-134호
주 소 | 서울시 도봉구 도봉로 180길 20 투웨니퍼스트 102동 602호
전 화 | 02)2266-8606
팩 스 | 02)2266-8607
E-mail | jisikin2013@naver.com

ISBN 979-11-88105-43-4 (93740)

값 10,000원

English for Global Communication

Tourist Information & Creative Thinking for Language Learners

CONTENTS

China

CHAPTER 1

About China

Unit 1

Vocabulary & Grammar Practice

[1] Which of the following best completes the sentences?

The weather in China is extremely various. Great differences in climate are found from region to region owing to China's (   ) territory and complex topography.

a) intensive
b) extensive
c) high
d) narrow

[2] Unscramble the words to find the correct definitions for the words below.

a) southernmost: south, farthest

➜

b) ethnic: of, race

➜

c) diverse: kind, a, of, different

➜

d) population: number, area, people, a particular, living, of, in

➜

e) census: population, process, official, country's, of, an, counting, a

➜

f) aesthetic: beauty, connected, with

➜

g) substantial: amount or number, enough, large, noticeable, in, to, be

➜

h) territory: land, district, or

➜

i) topography: the river, road, building, position, etc., of

➜

j) temperate: extremes, free, from

➜

Reading or Listening Practice

[1] Think about the following questions.

1. Name the countries around China.

___

2. Name the different peoples that make up China's population.

___

3. What is the major religion in China?

___

4. What is the major language in China?

___

5. Name the tourist attractions in China.

___

[2] Read or listen to the following passages and answer the above questions.

China is located in Eastern Asia, bordering the East China Sea, Korea Bay, Yellow Sea, and South China Sea, between North Korea and Vietnam. China is slightly smaller than the United States and is the world's fourth-largest country after Russia, Canada, and US. In China, there are 6,536 islands larger than 500 square meters, the largest being Taiwan, and the second largest is Hainan. The majority of China's people live in the eastern segment of the country.

China is a country with 56 nationalities, including the Han, the Manchu, the Mongol, the Uygur, the Zhuang, the Tibetan and so on. China's ethnically diverse population is the largest in the world. China was a nation of about one-fifth of the world's populations. These nationalities are distributed all over China and form diversified folk cultures due to the varying natural and social environment they live in. The Han people make up over 90 percent of the total population. Different ethnic groups usually follow different religions, so China is a multi-religious country. Buddhism, Taoism and Islam are the three major religions. Catholicism and Protestantism have smaller but substantial followers, too. On the whole, however, religion has not been a major issue in China.

In languages, both Putonghua (the dialect of Mandarin as spoken in Beijing) and English are the languages of business. So, if the foreigners travel to China for business purposes, they can usually communicate with the Chinese merchants in simple English. However, Putonghua is an official language of China. Most of the Chinese merely speak Putonghua with the outsiders. So, if the foreign tourists want to visit China but cannot speak Putonghua, they will find traveling in China inconvenient.

The weather in China is extremely diverse. Great differences in climate are found from region to region owing to China's extensive territory and complex topography. Although most of the country lies in the temperate zone, southern areas are in the tropical or subtropical zone while northern areas are in the frigid zone. In general, the temperature in China in the winter is 5 to 18 degrees centigrade lower than that in other countries on the same latitude in winter.

There are many tourist attractions in China. Beijing has been the capital city of China since the Ming dynasty (1368-1644). After more than 700 years, the historical sites – the Forbidden City, the Temple of Heaven, the Summer Palace and the Great Wall are still maintained in good shape. Shanghai, the largest city of China, is located on the east coast of China and is the gateway of the Yangze River basin. For centuries Shanghai has been a comprehensive industrial base and an important port for China-international trade. Hong Kong became the Special Administrative Region (SAR) of China on 1 July 1997. Despite the change of leadership from British rule to Chinese, Hong Kong remains one of the world's most important economic centers and one of the most popular vacation destinations on the earth.

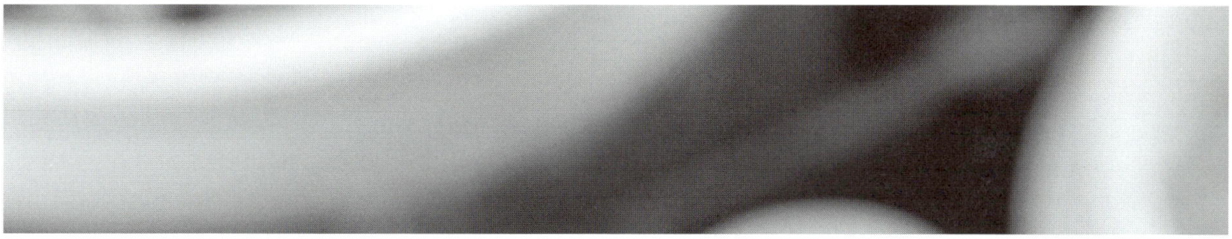

CHAPTER 1

China

Shopping & Dining in China

Unit 2

Vocabulary & Grammar Practice

[1] Which of the following is closest to the meaning of the underlined word?

Whereas foods from Canton are delicate, in Sichuan food the <u>tastes</u> are strong and dramatic

a) dishes
b) flavors
c) sauces
d) dressings

[2] Which of the following best completes the sentences?

Sichuan food is the (   ) food of China, where pepper and chili really get into the act

a) very sweet
b) very hot
c) very sour
d) very bitter

[3] Match each word in the first column with its meaning in the second column.

a) craft •	• a) a job needing skill, esp. with one's hands
b) inheritance •	• b) to make or become greater in number or quantity
c) embroidery •	• c) property you receive from someone who has died
d) pottery •	• d) to give something a different color using a dye
e) dyeing •	• e) a copy of a painting or other work of art
f) replica •	• f) a decoration or pattern made by sewing onto cloth
g) exquisitely •	• g) extremely beautifully, excellently
h) relic •	• h) object made out of baked clay
i) accumulate •	• i) something old that reminds us of the past
j) liquor •	• j) an alcoholic drink

Reading or Listening Practice

[1] Think about the following questions.

1. List products that can be purchased in China.

2. Name foods you can enjoy in China.

3. Write the key points, based on what you heard (read) from the below passages.

[2] Read or listen to the following passages and answer the above questions.

China is a treasure house of arts and crafts which are an important part of the Nation's cultural inheritance. Products such as carving, embroidery, pottery, dyeing, and replicas of ancient cultural relics are all exquisitely crafted. Other famous Chinese products include silk, tea, liquors and traditional Chinese medicine. China is also the home of tea. Tea is divided into green, black, perfumed, white and Wulong tea. Longjing (green tea) and Biluochun (green tea) are famous throughout the world. And China's liquors have developed in their own unique way and have won many international awards. There are many famous liquors such as Maotai. Traditional Chinese medicine is famous throughout the world as well. The body of knowledge that makes up traditional Chinese medicine has been accumulated over thousands of years.

Chinese food enjoys a high reputation in the world not only for its delicious taste and charming appearance but also for its abundance. It is due to the diversity of the climate, products and customs that there are widely different food styles and tastes in local regions. Beijing food is the most famous food of China, particularly known for Beijing (Peking) Duck. A Beijing Duck dinner is usually a fixed item on any Beijing tour itinerary. Cantonese food or Guangdong food, another famous food of China, typically is steamed, boiled or stir-fried. It is a very healthy food since it uses a minimum amount of oil. The main ingredients of this type of Chinese food are seafood, pork, chicken and vegetables, but could include almost anything. It is said, "the Cantonese eat every thing that flies except planes, every thing on the ground except cars, and every thing that is in water except boats." Sichuan food is the fiery food of China, where pepper and chili really get into the act. Whereas foods from Canton are delicate, in Sichuan food the flavors are strong and dramatic.

China
CHAPTER 1

Language Practice | Unit 3

How do you say the following in English?

1. 중국의 동해안에 위치해 있는 상하이는 중국에서 가장 인구가 많은 도시이다.

2. 명, 청 왕조 동안 황제의 궁전이었던 자금성은 세계에서 가장 큰 궁전이다.

3. 세계에서 가장 경이스러운 것 중에 하나로 여겨지는 만리장성은 유네스코에 의해 1987년에 세계문화유산에 등재되었다.

4. 중국에서 가장 잘 보존되어 있는 왕실 정원인 이하원은 예전에 청왕조 황제의 여름 거주지였다.

5. 중국인들은 비행기를 빼고 나는 모든 것을, 차를 제외하고 땅에 있는 모든 것을, 배를 빼고 물에 있는 모든 것을 먹는다고들 한다.

Incomplete Sentences

Choose the word or phrase that best completes the sentence.

1. *Every Sunday night I __________ the TV show 'I'm a singer' on MBC.*

a) watch b) watches
c) watched d) have watched

2. *The main conference room __________ in use since 8 a.m.*

a) have been b) is
c) was d) has been

3. *She seems to __________ the piano really hard this semester.*

a) has practiced b) have practiced
c) has been practiced d) have been practiced

4. *I __________ for my final exams these days and it has been stressful.*

a) has been studying b) have studied
c) have been studying d) will study

5. *Japan knows well the historical fact that Dokdo __________ Korea.*

a) is belonging to b) belong to
c) belongs to d) belongs

6. *The president __________ Russia's war victory anniversary next month.*

a) will not attend b) will not attended
c) will attend not d) will not be attended

7. *Korean TV dramas and pop music __________ more popular in Peru.*

a) is becoming b) to become
c) are becoming d) becoming

8. *The company __________ financially in recent years.*

a) have been struggling
b) has been struggling
c) had been struggling
d) has been struggled

9. *She was angered at how nuts __________ by a flight attendant.*

a) has been served
b) had served
c) had been served
d) has served

10. *It is imperative that the meeting __________ at once, or we're never going to get out of here.*

a) beginning
b) begins
c) began
d) begin

11. *The flight attendant __________ the school children according to the order they arrived on the plane.*

a) sit
b) sat
c) seated
d) seat

12. *Those in their 50s __________ retirement.*

a) are soon faced
b) are soon facing
c) is soon facing
d) is soon faced

13. *When I got there, it __________ for three days.*

a) had been raining
b) has been raining
c) is raining
d) had raining

14. *I can't believe that you __________ there for more than 45 minutes when she finally arrived.*

a) had been standing
b) stood
c) did stand
d) has been standing

Incomplete Texts

Choose the best word or phrase for each blank.

Questions 1 through 3 refer to the following e-mail.

To: Mary
From: Rita
Re: Send report again

Hi!

I found the report that you attached to your e-mail when I ____________ on to my

1. a) loged
   b) logged
   c) log
   d) was logged

computer this morning. I __________ the report was great. I wanted to keep it, so I

2. a) though
   b) think
   c) thought
   d) through

tried to save it to my hard disk. Unfortunately, I clicked on the wrong button and I deleted it instead! I tried to undo the command, but that didn't work. So I searched for it, but it just wasn't there. Could you __________ it again?

3. a) sent
   b) be sent
   c) send
   d) be sending

Thank you.

Questions 4 through 6 refer to the following advertisement.

TODAY ONLY

Attention Customers!

Come one, come all. Step right up. For the next 4 hours we are __________ a special on

4. a) have
   b) having
   c) had
   d) will have

all items with a blue tag on them. For those of you with quick feet, the first 25 customers to purchase one of our blue tag items will receive a free gift. And for a special treat we have Gizmo the clown set up outside in our pink Jell-O dunk tank. If you purchase 5 blue tag items today, we __________ 5 free tickets to our dunk tank.

5. a) included
   b) including
   c) did include
   d) will include

So if you have any small children, or a fear of clowns that you need to deal with, please feel free to buy as many of our blue tag items as you can carry.
Also, don't forget to check out our every day low prices on household items like Perrie-Air canned fresh air, Bluth's Frozen Bananas, Slurm cola and Diet Slurm, Mr. Coffee ___________ containers, Mr. Fusion Energy bars, Hover-boards, and Blitz Lightyear

6. a) refilling
   b) refillable
   c) re-filed
   d) filled

action figures. Buy any of these items now and receive a free coupon for a Pizza Planet restaurant near you.

CHAPTER 2

Thailand

About Thailand | Unit 1

Vocabulary & Grammar Practice

[1] **Which of the following is closest to the meaning of the underlined word?**

> There are three seasons: the cool season from November to February, the hot season from April to May, and the rainy season from June to October, though downpours rarely <u>continue</u> more than a couple of hours.

a) stop
b) happen
c) last
d) comprise

[2] **Unscramble the words to find the correct definitions for the words below.**

a) infertile: of, incapable, producing
→

b) rural: a countryside, of
→

c) urban: a town or city, of
→

d) fertile: to produce, able, crops, good
→

e) counterfeit: that, to look like, is made, the original one, something
→

f) celadon: a pale green glaze, pottery, a type, having, of
→

g) cuisine: cooking, of, a style
→

h) vendor: things, sells, who, someone
→

i) gem: a special shape, into, cut, has been, that, a beautiful stone
→

j) arid: dry, extremely
→

Reading or Listening Practice

[1] Think about the following questions.

1. Name the countries around Thailand.

____

2. Which months are best for sightseeing in Thailand?

____

3. Name the different peoples that make up Thailand's population.

____

4. What is the major language in Thailand?

____

5. What is the major religion in Thailand?

____

[2] Read or listen to the following passages and answer the above questions.

A unified Thai kingdom was established in the mid-14th century. It was known as Siam until 1939 and it boasts the distinction of being the only country in Southeast Asia never to have been colonized by a European power. The word "Thai" means "free," and therefore "Thailand" means "Land of the Free."

Geographically, the Kingdom of Thailand is located in the heart of Southeast Asia and shares boundaries with Myanmar (Burma) on the west and northwest, Laos on the east and northeast, Cambodia on the southeast, and Malaysia on the south. It comprises the flat, damp plains of the Chao Phraya river estuary, ideal for growing rice.

Lying within the humid tropics, Thailand remains hot throughout the year.

Average low temperature is about 20℃ and high temperature is 37℃. There are three seasons: the cool season from November to February, the hot season from April to May, and the rainy season from June to October, though downpours rarely last more than a couple of hours. The best time to go is from November through February, when the days are milder and the nights are cool.

The diversity of ethnic, linguistic, and religious groups is characteristic of most nations of Southeast Asia. However, Thailand's population is relatively homogeneous. More than 85% speak a dialect of Thai and share a common culture. Ethnic Thais form the majority. The largest minority is Chinese. Other minority groups include Malays, Cambodians, Indians, non-Thai hill tribes, and some Vietnamese.

The official national language of Thailand is Thai. Thai is a tone language. This means that different tones have different meanings. The Thai language has five tones, and if you mispronounce you do not simply say an incorrect word, you say another word entirely. Principal other languages are Chinese and Malay. English is a mandatory subject in public schools, and widely spoken and understood particularly in Bangkok and other major cities.

Thailand is one of the most strongly Buddhist countries in the world. Buddhism continues to cast strong influence on daily life. Every Thai male is expected to become a monk for a short period in his life, optimally between the time he finishes school and the time he starts a career or marries. The remainder of the population adheres to Islam, Christianity, Hinduism, and other faiths – all of which are allowed full freedom of expression.

Thailand is an easy country to travel in, with efficient transport, inexpensive accommodations and a delicious national cuisine. The Thais are renowned for their friendliness and hospitality to strangers. Thailand is equally well known for both its beach resorts and the shopping and night life of its busy cities. Popular destinations include the capital Bangkok, Chiangmai, and the resorts in Phuket, Koh Samui and Pattaya.

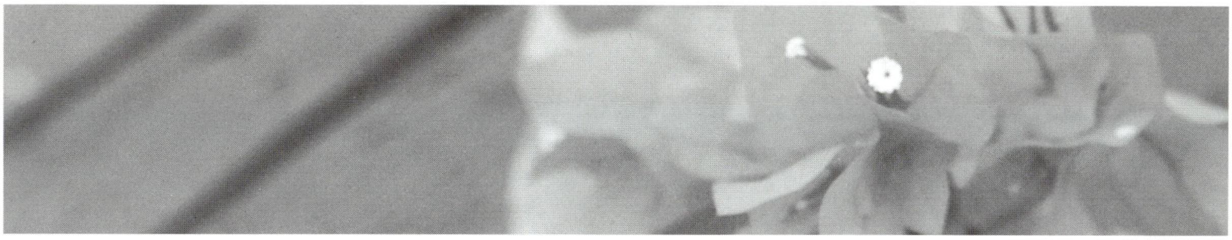

CHAPTER 2

Thailand

Shopping & Dining in Thailand

Unit 2

Vocabulary & Grammar Practice

[1] Which of the following best completes the sentences?

Thailand owes its rich culinary arts to the (   ) of India, China, Malaysia and Indonesia.

a) cuisines
b) music
c) painting
d) religion

[2] Which of the following best completes the sentences?

The success of this country's cuisine lies in the (   ) of 4 basic tastes i.e. salty, sweet, sour and pungent.

a) mixture
b) pleasure
c) cuisine
d) cook

[3] Match each word in the first column with its meaning in the second column.

a) indigenous •	• a) native
b) virtually •	• b) almost, very nearly
c) gem •	• c) imitator
d) counterfeit •	• d) copy, imitation
e) copycat •	• e) a copy of a shape made by rubbing wax onto a piece of paper laid over
f) lacquer •	• f) vessels and other objects made of baked clay
g) celadon •	• g) a type of pottery having a pale green glaze
h) pottery •	• h) varnish used to give a hard, bright coating to metal
i) handicraft •	• i) work needing skill with the hands and artistic design
j) rubbing •	• j) jewel

Reading or Listening Practice

[1] **Think about the following questions.**

1. *List products that can be purchased in Thailand.*

2. *Name foods you can enjoy in Thailand.*

3. *Write the key points, based on what you heard (read) from the below passages.*

[2] Read or listen to the following passages and answer the above questions.

Generally, shopping in Thailand is easy and fun. Bangkok is the colored gemstone capital of the world. Rubies and sapphires are indigenous stones, but virtually all colored gems, as well as diamonds, are available. Silk is a great buy in Bangkok, but there are a variety of qualities available. Other good shopping bargains are lacquer ware, celadon pottery, painted umbrellas, tribal weavings and handicrafts, temple rubbings, custom-made shoes and clothing, bronze, silver, gems, and temple bells. Bargaining is common in markets and with street vendors, but not in shops.

Thai food is internationally famous. Thailand owes its rich culinary arts to the cuisines of India, China, Malaysia and Indonesia. The success of this country's cuisine lies in the blend of 4 basic tastes i.e. salty, sweet, sour and pungent. Most dishes are masterfully balanced: They are hot, sweet, sour and spicy – all at the same time. The variety of vegetable and meat dishes is astonishing. Pork, poultry and some beef are used and seafood is outstanding.

Thailand is a paradise for tropical fruits. At any time during the year at least a dozen different kinds of fruits can be found in the market. These include the durians, rambutans, and mangosteens. Rambutans with soft spines on the outside taste like a sweet lemon. The mangoes are good in March through July. Mangosteens are another great-tasting tropical fruit. They are round with dark-brown skin, and are a little bigger than a golf ball. Inside is a sweet white fruit in segments, like an orange. Papayas and pomelos like a sweet grapefruit are also available. And if you can get past the smell, try the infamous durian fruit (It's so pungent that it's illegal to open one in your hotel room). There are more than 20 kinds of bananas. Thais eat them fresh, grilled and fried.

CHAPTER 2

Thailand

Language Practice | Unit 3

How do you say the following in English?

1. 시암(Siam)으로 알려진 태국은 동남아시아의 중앙에 위치한다.

2. 태국의 수도로 설립된 방콕은 지리적으로 경제적으로 그 나라의 심장부이다.

3. 태국에서 가장 큰 여행지 중의 하나인 파타야(Pattaya)는 수상스포츠에 이상적인 곳이다.

4. 태국에서 가장 큰 섬인 Phuket은 관광하기에 아주 매력적이다.

5. 테마파크인 Mini Siam에는 태국의 역사 유적과 사원의 축척 모형이 있다.

Incomplete Sentences

Choose the word or phrase that best completes the sentence.

1. *__________ the possibility of rain tomorrow, the event will go ahead as planned.*

   a) Despite b) While
   c) Aside d) Although

2. *The scheduled presentation for today at 1 p.m. has been postponed __________ next Friday.*

   a) by b) until
   c) still d) ago

3. *You should not talk to strangers here __________ you are spoken to.*

   a) unless b) if
   c) because d) although

4. *The meeting took place from March 10 __________ 13 in the main conference room.*

   a) though b) through
   c) on d) before

5. *Since __________ on Feb, 27, he has been working hard for the president.*

   a) took office b) take office
   c) he takes office d) taking office

6. *I met my friend in high school __________ lunch time.*

   a) during b) while
   c) for d) in

7. *She spent 20 million won on hotel bills __________ repairing her house.*

   a) for b) while
   c) during d) while she repairs

8. *Last year, 36,000 people lost a combined 216.5 billion won __________ voice phishing fraud.*

a) because
b) in spite of
c) despite
d) due to

9. *__________ he nor I am going to the restaurant tonight.*

a) Neither
b) Either
c) Both
d) Not only

10. *As soon as you __________ the bell, you have to go out and wait for your teacher.*

a) will hear
b) is going to hear
c) is hearing
d) hear

11. *They offer goods __________ competitive prices.*

a) on
b) in
c) at
d) up

12. *__________, the police officer could face up to 10 years in prison.*

a) If convicted
b) If convicting
c) If conviction
d) If he is convicting

13. *He disappeared __________ leaving a suicide note at his home.*

a) before
b) while
c) during
d) after

14. *After he __________ his job, he'd like to spend more time with his grandchildren.*

a) will quit
b) quits
c) quit
d) am quitted

Incomplete Texts

Choose the best word or phrase for each blank.

Questions 1 through 3 refer to the following advertisement.

SKYFARI AERIAL TRAM

Sponsored by Delta Air Lines.
Transportation and spectacular views over the treetops to ________________ of the Zoo.

1. a) the others side
   b) other side
   c) others side
   d) the other side

Tickets and departures from two terminals: east terminal is __________ the main entrance,

2. a) left of
   b) left in
   c) left to
   d) left on

______________ the Reptile House; west terminal is next to the Polar Bear Plunge.

3. a) cross from
   b) across from
   c) cross to
   d) across to

Please be advised that children under age 8 must be accompanied by an adult. Limit four riders per gondola. Open daily from 10 a.m. East terminal closes at 9:15 p.m. west terminal closes at 9:30 p.m.

Questions 4 through 6 refer to the following news report.

Asian's Budget Carrier Plan Stalls

Asian Airlines plans to set up a low-cost carrier (LCC) this year, but it will not be easy. ______________________, an Asian plane from Incheon ran off the

4. a) In Tuesday night
   b) At Tuesday night
   c) On Tuesday night
   d) To Tuesday night

runway at Hiroshima airport. Of the 73 passengers and seven crew members, 27 sustained minor injures. Korean and Japanese authorities are investigating.

Asiana plans to set up Seoul Air by the end of the year. It wants to use Gimpo and Inchoen airports as Seoul Air's bases. It has to get a license from the Ministry of Land, Infrastructure and Transport. Market watchers expected the ministry to issue the license without major problems. __________, the Hiroshima

5. a) Because
   b) However
   c) Because of
   d) Due to

accident has raised concerns over its safety management abilities. ________ the

6. a) When
   b) Although
   c) Because of
   d) As

related law considers safety as the prime condition for the issue of a license, some forecast that the ministry may refuse or delay permission.

CHAPTER 3

Malaysia

About Malaysia | Unit 1

Vocabulary & Grammar Practice

[1] Which of the following best completes the sentences?

There are 8,000 (   ) of flowering plants in Peninsular Malaysia alone, including 2,000 tree species, 800 different orchids and 200 types of palm.

a) species
b) bunches
c) collection
d) community

[2] Unscramble the words to find the correct definitions for the words below.

a) tip: something, of, the end

→

b) strait: that, two seas, a narrow passage of water, links

→

c) merge: one thing, together, to form, join

→

d) crossroad: where, place, two roads, meet

→

e) carve: wood or stone, a shape, to cut, into

→

f) skewer: a piece of food, a hole, to make, through

→

g) concoction: a drink, different things, mixing, made, by

→

h) stall: an open front, a small shop, with

→

i) lamb: the flesh, lamb or sheep, of

→

j) utensil: a tool, in cooking, with a particular use

→

Reading or Listening Practice

[1] Think about the following questions.

1. Name the countries around Malaysia.

   ____

2. Name the different peoples that make up Malaysia's population.

   ____

3. What is the major religion in Malaysia?

   ____

4. What is the major language in Malaysia?

   ____

5. Name the tourist attractions in Malaysia.

   ____

[2] Read or listen to the following passages and answer the above questions.

Malaysia, located in the heart of Southeast Asia, is divided into two main regions: Peninsular Malaysia, which lies just south of Thailand, and East Malaysia, which can be found north of Indonesia on the island of Borneo. Geographically, it is the southernmost tip of the Asian mainland. Further South is Singapore, across the Straits of Johor. But there is more Malaysia eastwards beyond the South China Sea where the states of Sarawak and Sabah are located. Both these states are part of the world's third largest island – Borneo.

Malaysia, formed in 1963 through a merging of the former British colonies of Malaya and Singapore, is a multicultural society, with Malays, Chinese and Indians living side by side. The Malays are the largest community. They are

Muslims, speak Bahasa and are largely responsible for the political fortunes of the country. The Chinese comprise about a third of the population. The Indians account for about 10% of the population. They are mainly Hindu Tamis and they speak Tamil, Malayalam, and some Hindi, and live mainly in the larger towns on the west coast of the peninsula. Eurasians and indigenous tribes make up the remaining population.

Malaysia's national language is Bahasa Melayu (Malay language). Although Bahasa Melayu is the official language, the mother tongues of the other communities such as Hokkien, Hakka, Tamil, Mandarin, Bennggali and others are also widely spoken. The evolution of Manglish (Malaysian English) has taken a life of its own. It is not only confined to the use of the suffix 'lah', but is more pervasive than can be imagined. In practice, you'll be able to get by with English in almost all the areas in the country, since the language is often used as a means of communication between the races, as well as being the language of business.

The weather in Malaysia is tropical without extremely high temperatures. Days are very warm, while nights are fairly cool. Average temperature is between 21 to 32 degree Celsius. Humidity is high. Rain tends to occur between November to February on the east coast of Peninsular Malaysia, on western Sarawak, and north-eastern Sabah. On the west coast of Peninsular Malaysia the rainy seasons are April to May and October to November.

There are 8,000 species of flowering plants in Peninsular Malaysia alone, including 2,000 tree species, 800 different orchids and 200 types of palm. Fauna includes elephants, tigers, leopards, sun bears, orangutans and varied bird populations in the world. More than 60 percent of the country is still rainforest.

Malaysia is one of the most satisfying tourist destinations in the world. Popular destinations include Kuala Lumpur, Malacca, Johor Bahru, and so forth.

Malaysia

CHAPTER 3

Shopping & Dining in Malaysia

Unit 2

Vocabulary & Grammar Practice

[1] Which of the following is closest to the meaning of the underlined word?

Because Malaysia is a country of diverse cultures and traditions, it is not surprising that its <u>cuisine</u> is just as diverse.

a) food
b) economy
c) language
d) religion

[2] Which of the following best completes the sentences?

Most meals are eaten by using your (   ), while eating utensils are kept to a minimum.

a) fingers
b) chopsticks
c) knives
d) spoons

[3] Match each word in the first column with its meaning in the second column.

a) crossroad •	• a) to have the most importance or influence
b) brocade •	• b) making or inscribing by cutting
c) varied •	• c) decorative cloth usually of silk, often with a raised pattern of gold or silver threads
d) brass •	• d) place where two roads meet and cross each other
e) kite •	• e) various, diverse
f) carving •	• f) very hard bright yellow metal
g) household •	• g) to make a hole through a piece of food; an object with a skewer or with something similar
h) predominate •	• h) a young sheep; the meat of a young sheep
i) lamb •	• i) connected with looking after a house and the people in it
j) skewer •	• j) a wooden or metal frame covered with paper or cloth for flying in the air

Reading or Listening Practice

[1] Think about the following questions.

1. *List products that can be purchased in Malaysia.*

2. *Name foods you can enjoy in Malaysia.*

3. *Write the key points, based on what you heard (read) from the below passages.*

[2] Read or listen to the following passages and answer the above questions.

Malaysia is a shoppers' paradise. Since it is situated at the crossroads of Asia, it presents visitors the best that the region has to offer. Among the items high on the shopping list of tourists are batik, silverwork, gold and silver brocade, local handicrafts, kites and carvings. The variety of bargain items you can find in the major markets is endless, ranging from quality electronics to traditional arts and crafts. Kota Bharu is one of the best places to shop for handicrafts. Langkawi has duty-free areas with bargains on electronics, household goods and jewelry.

You could travel to Malaysia just to eat: The variety of food is incredible. Because Malaysia is a country of diverse cultures and traditions, it is not surprising that its cuisine is just as varied. Chinese, Indian and Malay cuisines predominate, though in restaurants in larger cities we've even had French and North African dishes. Some traditional Malay dishes include rendang (beef, lamb and chicken in coconut milk), satay (skewered meat in peanut sauce), pulut (various sticky- rice concoctions cooked inside a banana leaf), ikan bilis (dried anchovies fried in a sauce and served with rice) and murtabak (crepes stuffed with egg, meat and vegetables). Chicken, fish, noodles and curries are everywhere. Rice is the staple diet in any Malay meal. The Malaysian food is spicy, and coconut milk is a common ingredient. Authentic Malay food is not as widely available in Malaysian restaurants as Chinese style or American fast food. Restaurants in large hotels offer international cuisine from such countries as Japan, Korea, France and Italy. The street stalls offer delicious and cheap Malaysian food. Malaysia also offers a cornucopia of delicious tropical fruit: rambutan (similar to lychee), mangosteen (probably the best-tasting tropical fruit) and the infamous durian (undoubtedly the world's smelliest).

Malaysia

CHAPTER 3

Language Practice | Unit 3

How do you say the following in English?

1. 동남아시아의 심장부에 위치해 있는 말레이시아는 다문화 사회이다.

2. 말레이시아의 남쪽 끝에 위치한 Johor Bahru는 싱가포르와 방죽길로 연결되어 있다.

3. 동양의 진주로 알려진 Penang은 열대 섬 리조트이다.

4. 말라카(Malacca)에 있는 역사적 건물은 네덜란드인이 건축한 것이다.

5. 말레이시아는 중국인이 인구의 약 1/3을 차지한다.

Incomplete Sentences

Choose the word or phrase that best completes the sentence.

1. *Three types of bags are becoming ________ popular in New York.*

a) surprise b) surprised
c) surprising d) surprisingly

2. *Voice phishing fraud is a crime which makes people ________.*

a) anxious b) anxiety
c) anxiously d) anxiousness

3. *Mr. Sung was found ________ on Mt. Bukhan in an apparent suicide.*

a) died b) dead
c) die d) death

4. *Delson may be a small company, but its computers are ________ in quality.*

a) comparison b) comparative
c) compare d) comparable

5. *The money for the development project was spent ________, according to due procedures.*

a) transparently b) transparent
c) transparenting d) to transparent

6. *They are the subject of ________ international criticism.*

a) considerate b) consider
c) consideration d) considerable

7. *In December, he signed ________ extension with the publishing company.*

a) a two-years contract b) a two-year contract
c) a two-years contracts d) two-year contract

8. *The __________ organization will begin working at the beginning of the year.*

a) new launched
b) launched newly
c) newly launched
d) new launch

9. *I am proud to say that our product __________ for use.*

a) is safe
b) is safety
c) is safely
d) is safeness

10. *Ahn made __________ bold decisions for the company.*

a) much
b) little
c) a little
d) a few

11. *The problem is __________.*

a) new nothing
b) nothing new
c) newly nothing
d) nothing newly

12. *The NTOK(The National Theater of Korea) remained __________ for a long time.*

a) unchanged
b) unchange
c) to unchange
d) unchangely

13. *The risk of skin cancer can __________ by putting on sunscreen.*

a) be reduced significant
b) significantly reduce
c) be significantly reduced
d) reduce significantly

14. *__________ a year has passed since the sinking of the Sewel ferry.*

a) Near
b) Even
c) Early
d) Nearly

Incomplete Texts

Choose the best word or phrase for each blank.

Questions 1 through 3 refer to the memo.

To: All Customer Service Representatives
From: Director of Customer Service
Subject: Customer Service Handbook
Date: March 3, 2015

Memo

Attached is the new customer service handbook. Please take time and look at it ________________. There have been some changes in the handbook.

1. a) careful
   b) carefully
   c) care
   d) carefulness

It has two sections: Procedures and Strategies. You will find the policies that must be followed for ________________________ reasons in the Procedure section.

2. a) legal and financially
   b) legally and financially
   c) legally and financial
   d) legal and financial

When you discuss policies with a customer, be sure to give the reasons to them. Do not simply say, "Our policy is ..."
There are many useful ideas when you deal with a customer in the Strategies section. In order to help our customers in the future, please familiarize _______________ with both sections of the handbook.

3. a) yourself
   b) you
   c) your
   d) yours

Questions 4 through 6 refer to the following advertisement.

WORLD-FAMOUS SAN DIEGO ZOO

GENERAL INFORMATION

Open at 9 a.m., 365 days a year. Closing times vary by season. For __________ hours

4. a) currently
   b) currentness
   c) current
   d) currentnessly

and prices, please call (619) 234-3153.

Members of the Zoological Society of San Diego receive free admission for one year to the San Diego Zoo and San Diego Wild Animal Park. For __________ information

5. a) most
   b) many
   c) many more
   d) more

inquire at membership booth at main entrance or call (619) 231-0251.

Group rates and catered events are __________. Call (619) 675-7900.

6. a) available
   b) avail
   c) availably
   d) availablity

Prices and hours are subject to change without notice.

For panda viewing hours call toll-free 1-888-MYPANDA.

Located in Balboa Park, off Park Blvd. From Hwy 163, exit Park Blvd. and follow the signs. From 1-5, take the Pershing Drive exit and follow the signs.

CHAPTER 4

Singapore

About Singapore | Unit 1

Vocabulary & Grammar Practice

[1] Which of the following best completes the sentences?

It joined Malaysia in 1963, but withdrew two years later and became (   ).

a) dependent
b) independent
c) merged
d) inhibited

[2] Unscramble the words to find the correct definitions for the words below.

a) withdraw: away or back, to move
➜

b) uninhibited: action and behavior, in, free
➜

c) souvenir: an event, trip, place, etc., of, a reminder, as, kept, an object
➜

d) artifact: human beings, by, produced or shaped, an object
➜

e) curio: because it is old, beautiful, or rare, object, small, that is valuable
➜

f) suburbs: an area, a lot of people, the center of a town or city, where, away from, live
➜

g) outlet: a store, a particular manufacturer or wholesaler, the goods, that, of, sells
➜

h) retailer: someone, things, who, a shop, in, sells
➜

i) counter offer: offer made, somebody else, in reply to, an offer made by
➜

j) fragrant: a, smell, pleasant, having
➜

Reading or Listening Practice

[1] Think about the following questions.

1. Name the countries around Singapore.

____

2. Which months are best for sightseeing in Singapore?

____

3. Name the different peoples that make up Singapore's population.

____

4. What is the major language in Singapore?

____

5. What is the major religion in Singapore?

____

[2] Read or listen to the following passages and answer the above questions.

Founded as a British trading colony in 1819, Singapore consists of the main island of Singapore and more than 50 smaller islands. It is a small, stable, and highly developed island country. It joined Malaysia in 1963, but withdrew two years later and became independent. About half of the smaller islands of Singapore are uninhibited. Some of the islands have been developed for recreation and tourism.

Singapore is shaped almost like a diamond. It is located at the southern tip of the Malay Peninsular, connected by a 1-kilometer-long causeway. Singapore's immediate neighbors are Malaysia, Brunei, Darussalam and Indonesia. Being very close to the equator, Singapore's climate is characterized by abundant rainfall, relatively uniform temperature and high humidity throughout the year. Singapore is wettest from November to January and is driest from May to July. The difference between the two is barely visible. June and August are claimed to be the best time to visit, but even then it rains often. When it dose rain, it's generally only for a short period every day. Light summer clothing should be worn.

Singapore is a multi-cultural city. Diversity is the key to Singapore's population: Chinese, Malay, Indonesia and others. Each area has its own culture celebrating its own religion. Due to many ethnic groups, Singapore has a dazzling range of languages. The official languages in Singapore are Malay, Chinese (Mandarin), Tamil and English. Malay is the national language and English is the language of administration and business. Most people are bilingual from infancy and it is common for people to know and use four or five languages in their daily life. Naturally the presence of other languages has influenced the English of Singapore. The influence is especially apparent in the kind of English that is used informally, which is popularly called Singlish. As most Singaporeans use a lot of Singaporean colloquial English to their children, children tend to speak Singaporean colloquial English.

The diversity of religions existed in Singapore is an outcome of various nationalities residing there. More than half of the Singapore's population are the followers of Buddhism and Taoism. The statistical fact about Singapore indicates that Chinese people are the largest ethnic group in Singapore, so there leaves no doubt why they are Buddhists or Taoists as these two religions were originally brought with them from China. But later some of them proselytized to Christianity influenced by the arrival of the Raffles. Most of Singapore's Indians are Hindus, though some of them are Muslims.

Tourism in Singapore offers you a multitude of tourist activities. There are destinations as diverse as marine parks, zoo gardens, museums and the famous Sentosa as well as the Singapore Isles.

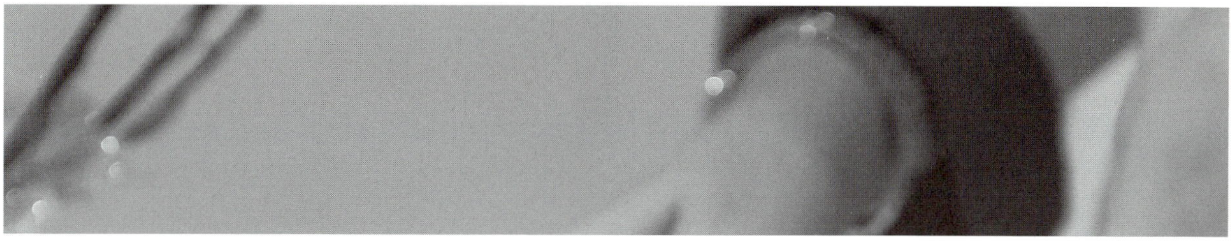

CHAPTER 4

Singapore

Shopping & Dining in Singapore

Unit 2

Vocabulary & Grammar Practice

[1] Which of the following is closest to the meaning of the underlined word?

> Fixed prices are the rule at department stores and at an increasing number of other outlets.

a) Set b) Cheap

c) Bargaining d) Expensive

[2] Which of the following best completes the sentences?

> When bargaining in a flexible-price store, begin by asking the retailer for his 'best price' and then make your (   ) offer.

a) nice b) counter

c) active d) low

[3] Match each word in the first column with its meaning in the second column.

a) souvenir •	• a) small object that is valuable because it is old, beautiful, or rare
b) artifact •	• b) an area away from the center of a town or city, where a lot of people live
c) curio •	• c) someone who sells things in a shop
d) suburbs •	• d) an object produced or shaped by human beings
e) ambience •	• e) having a pleasant smell
f) outlet •	• f) an object kept as a reminder of an event, trip, place etc.
g) retailer •	• g) offer made in reply to an offer made by somebody else
h) counter offer •	• h) environment; atmosphere
i) fragrant •	• i) grill
j) broil •	• j) a store that sells the goods of a particular manufacturer or wholesaler

Reading or Listening Practice

[1] Think about the following questions.

1. *List products that can be purchased in Singapore.*

2. *Name foods you can enjoy in Singapore.*

3. *Write the key points, based on what you heard (read) from the below passages.*

[2] Read or listen to the following passages and answer the above questions.

Singapore may be one of the smallest countries in size, but it is big on shopping. Souvenirs of Singapore can be found all over town in major department stores, shops and hotel shopping arcades. They range from T-shirts to local handicraft items. Health-giving ginseng can be found at Chinese medical halls all over Singapore. The city is also an international marketplace of jewelry, sporting goods, fashions, watches, cameras, electronics, Asian artifacts and curios. The most internationally famous shopping district in Singapore is the Orchard Road shopping belt. Fixed prices are the rule at department stores and at an increasing number of other outlets. Bargaining is mostly confined to smaller stores.

The food of Singapore reflects its multiethnic society. Almost every major international cuisine can be found in Singapore, with hundreds of restaurants dotted around the island. Chinese contributes to 10 percent of the population in Singapore, hence Chinese cuisine is one of the most popular cuisine in Singapore. Indian and Malayan dishes are also available. Chinese dishes include Char Kewy Teow (fried noodles), Popiah (fresh spring rolls) and Chicken Rice while Malay dishes include Nasi Lemak (fragrant rice in coconut milk) and Satay (skewered meat broiled over red-hot coals and dipped in peanut sauce).

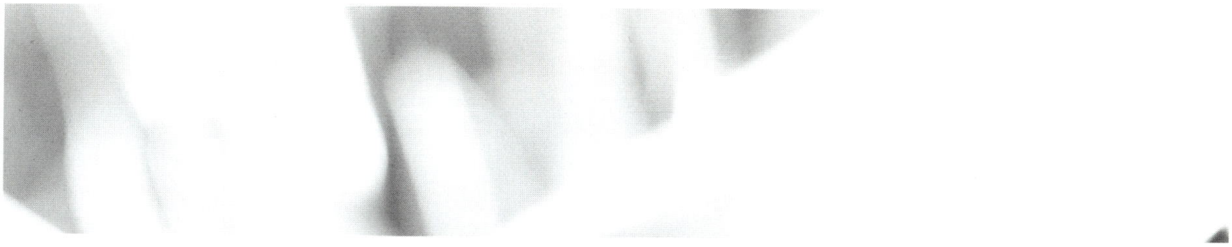

CHAPTER 4

Singapore

Language Practice | Unit 3

How do you say the following in English?

1. 싱가포르에서는 사람들이 4개 언어를 사용하는 것이 흔하다.

2. Clarke Quay는 식사, 쇼핑, 그리고 오락을 결합하고 있는 싱가포르의 강가 마을이다.

3. Sentosa 섬은 매년 수많은 방문객을 끌어 들이는 싱가포르의 거대한 테마공원이다.

4. Underwater World는 아시아의 가장 흥미 있는 열대 수족관으로 칭송 받고 있다.

5. 아시아의 가장 흥미 있는 열대 수족관으로 칭송받고 있는 Underwater World에는 80 미터의 투명한 터널이 있다.

Incomplete Sentences

Choose the word or phrase that best completes the sentence.

1. *His wedding invitations __________ entirely from recycled materials.*

a) are sent
b) are written
c) are made
d) are handed

2. *The suspect __________ guilty by the jury.*

a) was discovered
b) was rebuked
c) was acquitted
d) was found

3. *He __________ the company to agree to the contract terms.*

a) was demanded
b) demanded
c) was urged
d) urged

4. *The prosecution __________ issue a summons this week for him.*

a) is expected to
b) is expected
c) is expect to
d) expect to

5. *Two people __________ and the remainder __________ to prison camps.*

a) were executed - sent
b) executed - sent
c) executed - were sent
d) were executed - were sent

6. *The sinking of the ferry __________ on April 16th last year.*

a) was taken place
b) took place
c) took part in
d) has taken place

7. *He __________ five years in a jail because of taking bribes.*

a) was sentenced
b) was sentenced with
c) sentenced to
d) was sentenced to

8. *The foundation __________ receiving bribes.*

a) accused of
b) is accused in
c) accuse of
d) is accused of

9. *You __________ at work on time every morning.*

a) should be arrived
b) should have been arrived
c) should have arrived
d) should arrive

10. *Only a few civic groups __________ provide humanitarian aid.*

a) have been allowed to
b) have been allowing to
c) have allowed to
d) have allowing to

11. *The accident __________ on March 13 as one of the elevators stopped on the 13th floor.*

a) was happened
b) has been happened
c) happened
d) happens

12. *Kim __________ death last Friday at a hospital in Beijing.*

a) was pronounced
b) were pronounced
c) was pronounce
d) have been pronounced

13. *The movie theater __________ as a two-story wooden building in 1907.*

a) first built
b) has first been built
c) is first built
d) was first built

14. *He __________ a Korean mother and an African-American father in 1985.*

a) was born to
b) is born to
c) was born with
d) born to

Incomplete Texts

Choose the best word or phrase for each blank.

Questions 1 through 3 refer to the following new article.

NK seeks to enhance English education

North Korea is seeking to increase the use of English in school curricula, according to the North's weekly magazine. A report ______________ by the

1. a) published
   b) is published
   c) was published
   d) was publishing

North's Education Newspaper on April 2. It introduced ways to encourage the use of foreign language in teaching classes. "Basic words in the textbook should ______________ in English in parallel with Korean. Then, students can pay more

2. a) be written
   b) be writing
   c) write
   d) is written

attention to learning English words when studying their major," the report said. It said such teaching methods will help students read ______________ with

3. a) English-writing books
   b) English-written books
   c) English-write books
   d) English-wrote books

more confidence. The report came amid Pyongyang's active approach toward foreign language education.

Pyongyang's Education Committee has recently included English listening and conversation tests on the university entrance exam and exams to enter upper level schools.

Questions 4 through 6 refer to the following notice.

From: The Korea Times and the Northest Asian History Foundation
To: People from all over the world
Sub: Essay Contest

The 6th International Peace Essay Contest

The Korea Times and the Northeast Asian History Foundation invite you to participate in an English-language essay contest. The aim of the contest is to explore a healthy perception of history and ways to promote peace in Northeast Asia. Applicants ________________ to submit an essay of about 800 words on the

4. a) required
   b) require
   c) is required
   d) are required

theme, "How should we look back at history on the 70th anniversary of the end of World War II?"
Twelve winners _________________________. The Gold Prize winner will receive 1.5

5. a) will be selected
   b) are selected
   c) will be selecting
   d) will be been selected

million won, two silver Prize winners will each receive 500,000 won, and three Bronze Prize winners will each receive 300,000 won. Six will receive honorable mentions and 50,000 won.
The winning essays ________________________ in The Korea Times and a booklet.

6. a) will publish
   b) will be publishing
   c) will be published
   d) will be been published

If you need any further information, please call (02) 345-7845 or send an email kim@koreatimes.co.kr.
Please send your essay now!
Deadline for submissions: July 15, 2015
Announcement of winning entries: Aug 17, 2015
Awards Ceremony: Sep 3, 2015

CHAPTER 5

Indonesia

About Indonesia | Unit 1

Vocabulary & Grammar Practice

[1] Which of the following is closest to the meaning of the underlined word?

Indonesia is the largest country in Southeast Asia, the largest group of islands in the world, and is best known for its numerous island resorts peppered across the archipelago.

a) land
b) continent
c) archipelago
d) ocean

[2] Unscramble the words to find the correct definitions for the words below.

a) peak: sharply, pointed, mountain, top, a

➜

b) leather: animal, skin, shoes, bags, etc., used, treated, making, for

➜

c) archipelago: many, islands, of, group

➜

d) encompass: all, sides, surround, on, to

➜

e) landscape: country, scenery, a, view, wide, of

➜

f) migrate: to move, to, from, one place, another

➜

g) mosque: Muslims, worship, a building, in, which

➜

h) plantation: crops, grown, land, piece, of, a large, are, where

➜

i) monsoon: India and neighboring countries, the heavy rains, fall, in, which

➜

j) deter: acting, from, prevent, to

➜

Reading or Listening Practice

[1] Think about the following questions.

1. Name the countries around Indonesia.
____

2. Which months are best for sightseeing in Indonesia?
____

3. Name the peoples that make up Indonesia's population.
____

4. What is the major language in Indonesia?
____

5. What is the major religion in Indonesia?
____

[2] Read or listen to the following passages and answer the above questions.

Indonesia is the largest country in Southeast Asia, the largest archipelago in the world, and is best known for its numerous island resorts peppered across the archipelago. Of these, Bali, Lombok and Bintan are the most popular. Encompassing a large area between Australia and Asia, Indonesia is New Zealand's closest Asian neighbour. The Indonesian archipelago, comprising more than 13,000 islands, shares borders with Malaysia and Papua New Guinea and sea border with Singapore, Thailand, Vietnam, the Philippines and Australia.

The name Indonesia has its roots in two Greek words : "Indos" meaning Indian and "Nesos" which means islands. Indonesia's natural landscape ranges from rain forest and lush grasslands, to volcanic peaks and semi-desert. Under

10 percent of the total land area is suitable for farming, while two-thirds consists of woodland, forests and mangrove swamp. The main islands include Java, Sumatra, Sulawesi, Bali, Kalimantan, Nusa Tenggara, Maluku, and Irian Jaya.

Because Indonesia is situated around the equator the climate is tropical, hot and humid and is more moderate in the highlands. Humidity is between 60 and 100 percent. Though travel in the wet season is possible in most parts of Indonesia, it can be a deterrent to some activities and travel on mud-clogged roads in less developed areas is difficult. In general, the best time to visit is in the dry season between May and October.

There are a lot of ethnic divisions in Indonesia mostly split up by the separated islands but due to migration projects the ethnic groups are found all over the nation. From the total population 45% are Javanese, 14% are Sundanese, 7.5% are Madurese, 7.5% are coastal Malays and 26% belong to other ethnic groups. Due to the multi-ethnic divisions, over 300 languages are spoken in the archipelago and most belong to the Malay-Polynesian group. Within this group, many regional languages and dialects are spoken. On the island of Alor alone there are about 70 dialects and on Sulawesi 62 languages were identified. Still to be explored is Irian Jaya where till now more than 300 languages were found. Bahassa Indonesia or Indonesian is the official national language now. In all tourist destination areas English is the number one foreign language fairly spoken and written, whereas some Dutch is still spoken and understood in the bigger cities and French increasing in its popularity at the better hotels and restaurants.

The majority of the population (about 85%) are Moslems, ten percent are Christians, two percent are Hindus, and three percent are either Buddhists or animists. However, Churches, Hindu and Buddhist temples are found throughout the country, as are mosques of the Moslem faith.

CHAPTER 5

Indonesia

Shopping & Dining in Indonesia

Unit 2

Vocabulary & Grammar Practice

[1] Which of the following is closest to the meaning of the underlined word?

Bargaining is customary in small shops and markets, the art of which is to start at half the asking price and slowly increase your offer until a <u>settlement</u> is reached.

a) compromise

b) comprehension

c) conflict

d) decision

[2] Which of the following best completes the sentences?

Other craft forms include ikat, (   ) is a type of weaving with tie-dyed threads.

a) that

b) who

c) which

d) what

[3] Match each word in the first column with its meaning in the second column.

a) leather •	• a) treated animal skin used for making shoes, bags, etc.
b) apply •	• b) a solid material made out of fats or oils used to make candles
c) wax •	• c) to walk slowly for pleasure
d) customary •	• d) having a pleasant or acceptable taste
e) compromise •	• e) to lay one thing on or in another
f) stroll •	• f) usual, habitual
g) flock •	• g) the act of settling an argument by each side taking a middle course acceptable to all sides
h) palatable •	• h) a large piece of land, esp. in hot countries, on which crops such as tea, sugar, and rubber are grown
i) seasonal •	• i) happening or active at a particular season
j) plantation •	• j) a group of sheep, goats, or birds; a crowd; to gather in large crowds

Reading or Listening Practice

[1] Think about the following questions.

1. *List products that can be purchased in Indonesia.*

2. *Name foods you can enjoy in Indonesia.*

3. *Write the key points, based on what you heard (read) from the below passages.*

[2] Read or listen to the following passages and answer the above questions.

Indonesia is one of the world's shopping paradises. You can shop for batiks, silver, cloth, porcelain, wood and leather goods. The exact list is varied by location. Batik, the art of applying wax to cloth and the tie-dying in colorful and dramatic designs is produced throughout Indonesia, and has become high fashion in recent years. Today shops are available at a large variety of shopping centers and malls, providing international shopping environment with something to excite the whole family. People are now flocking to Indonesia to shop for very good reasons.

For most Indonesian people, a meal consists of steamed white rice with side dishes of meat, chicken, fish and vegetables along with a glass of tea. However, each province or area has its own cuisine, which varies in the method of cooking and ingredients. In Bali, Irian Jaya and the highlands of North Sumatra and North Sulawesi pork dishes are specialities. As the population of Indonesia is predominantly Moslem, pork is usually not served except in Chinese restaurants, non-Moslem regions and in places serving international cuisine. Chinese restaurants are found all over the country. There is such a rich variety in the Indonesian cuisine that one should sample specialities in each area. However, most common nationwide are "sate" (skewered grilled meat), "gado-gado" (vegetables salad with a peanut sauce), "nasi goreng" (fried rice served at anytime) and "bakmi goreng" (fried noodles).

There is also a wide variety of tropical and sub-tropical vegetables all year round. Fruit is available throughout the year. Some fruits such as mangoes and water melons are seasonal, but most of the other fruits can be bought throughout the whole year, such as bananas, apples, papayas, pineapples, oranges, etc. Coffee and tea plantations are plentiful, growing on several islands, and served everywhere from fine restaurants to small village stalls.

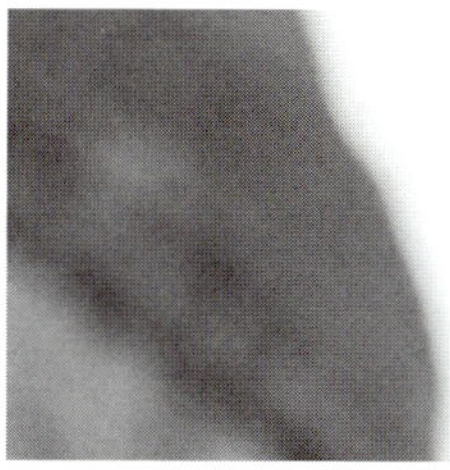

CHAPTER 5

Language Practice | Unit 3

How do you say the following in English?

1. 세계에서 가장 큰 군도인 인도네시아는 동남아시아에서 가장 큰 나라이다.

2. 인도네시아는 적도 부근에 위치해 있다.

3. 인도네시아의 인구는 압도적으로 회교도이다.

4. 인도네시아에서는 중국 음식점을 전역에 볼 수 있다.

5. Bali는 힌두교에 기반을 두고 있다.

Incomplete Sentences

Choose the word or phrase that best completes the sentence.

1. *The government agreed to a ________ bill supporting the project.*
   - a) revising
   - b) revise
   - c) revised
   - d) revisable

2. *The company estimated its quarterly ________ profit at 5.9 trillion won.*
   - a) operating
   - b) operate
   - c) operated
   - d) operation

3. *The ________ merger will facilitate the ongoing management shift.*
   - a) planning
   - b) plan
   - c) planed
   - d) planned

4. *North Korea has launched its first online shopping mall, the regime's ________ media reported Tuesday.*
   - a) state-controlled
   - b) state-control
   - c) state-controlling
   - d) state-controled

5. *________ the outcome of the negotiations, the company has no choice but to wait and see.*
   - a) Considered
   - b) Considering
   - c) Consider
   - d) Consideration

6. *Demand for low-tier smart phones remained strong in ________ countries.*
   - a) emerge
   - b) emergion
   - c) emerging
   - d) emerged

7. *Samsung faced ________ competition with Apple in the mobile division segment.*
   - a) heated
   - b) heating
   - c) heat
   - d) heater

8. *We're working closely with the ________ ministries to deal with the problem.*

a) relate　　b) related
c) relating　　d) relation

9. *The manager made ________ announcement at the meeting.*

a) an amazed　　b) a amazed
c) a amazing　　d) an amazing

10. *He denied his ________ involvement in covering up the crime.*

a) alleged　　b) alleging
c) allegation　　d) allegedly

11. *I would like to ________ with my friend this weekend.*

a) go shopping　　b) going shopping
c) go shop　　d) going shop

12. *________ by his wife, he went to the movies.*

a) Accompanying　　b) Accompany
c) Accompanied　　d) being accompanying

13. *Everyone knows that Ms. Lee is a hard ________ person.*

a) working　　b) worked
c) work　　d) being working

14. *I am ________ about my future.*

a) deeply worrying　　b) deep worrying
c) deep worried　　d) deeply worried

Incomplete Texts

Choose the best word or phrase for each blank.

Questions 1 through 3 refer to the following email.

To: Brenda Whitman
From: Sundar Pichai, Office Depot
Sub: Order reference #1234
Date: March 2nd

Dear Sir,

Thank you very much for your order of a Model 345 Laser Printer on February 25th. Unfortunately, it is out of stock right now. I called the manufacture and they said it is not available any more. Instead, we have several ___________ versions with many other

1. a) advancing
   b) advanced
   c) advance
   d) advancement

functions. I will send you some detailed _________ information on the products.

2. a) writing
   b) write
   c) written
   d) wrote

Please, read carefully the ___________ material and let me know if you need anything.

3. a) enclosed
   b) enclose
   c) enclosing
   d) enclosement

I am looking forward to hearing from you soon.
Thank you again.

Sincerely,
Sundar Pichai
Office Deport

Questions 4 through 6 refer to the following email.

From: Travel Agent
To: Jane Doe
Sub: Travel Destination

PALM SPRINGS

Dear Jane,

You asked me to recommend a beautiful place in California. I would like to introduce Palm Springs. There are two places to see: Palm Canyon and Twentynine Palms Oasis. Palm Canyon has been pictured in newspapers and magazine articles all over the world. It is one of the most ________________

4. a) outstanded
   b) outstand
   c) outstanding
   d) being outstand

spots in Palm Springs, California. This ____________ length of canyon

5. a) fifteen-mile
   b) fifteen-miles
   c) fifteen-miled
   d) fifteen-miling

wilderness is ______________. There is a combination of chaotic rocky gorges

6. a) breathtaken
   b) breathtaking
   c) breathtakingly
   d) breathtake

and minor canyons which are rough, barren and desertlike. An easy foot trail leads down into the canyon.
Twentynine Palms Oasis was known to the early Indians as the Oasis of Mara. It was called Twentynine Palms by Henry Washington in 1855. This group of palms stand guard at the gateway to the Joshus Tree National Monument.
If you have any more, please let me know.
Thank you.

CHAPTER 6

Philippines

About Philippines | Unit 1

Vocabulary & Grammar Practice

[1] Which of the following is closest to the meaning of the underlined word?

The 7000 islands that consist of the Philippines are the forgotten islands of South-East Asia.

a) comprehend

b) inhabit

c) immigrate

d) comprise

[2] Unscramble the words to find the correct definitions for the words below.

a) Filipino: the Philippines, of, a native or inhabitant

➜

b) Pilipino: language, the Filipino

➜

c) considerable: amount, size, or degree, in, fairly, large

➜

d) statue: wood, stone, bronze, etc., in, a person, animal, etc., of, figure

➜

e) occupy: to, a country, of, possession, take

➜

f) peel: the skin, off, to take

➜

g) profess: a religious order, of, the vows, to take

➜

h) cloth: material, weaving, by, formed

➜

i) instruction: teaching, of, the act or action

➜

j) traverse: across, pass

➜

Reading or Listening Practice

[1] Think about the following questions.

1. Name the countries around the Philippines.

   ____

2. Which months are best for sightseeing in the Philippines?

   ____

3. Name the different peoples that make up the Philippines's population.

   ____

4. What is the major religion in the Philippines?

   ____

5. What is the major language in the Philippines?

   ____

[2] Read or listen to the following passages and answer the above questions.

The Republic of the Philippines stands at the crossroads of the developed western world and the Orient. Taiwan, China and Hong Kong are northern neighbors and further north is Japan. To the west lie Southeast Asian countries such as Singapore, Malaysia and Thailand. Its three main islands are Luzon, Visayas and Mindanao.

It has a rich history combining Asian, European, and American influences. Prior to Spanish colonization in 1521, the Filipinos had a rich culture and were trading with the Chinese and the Japanese. The Philippines were ceded by Spain to the US in 1898 following the Spanish-American War. They attained their independence in 1946 after being occupied by the Japanese in World War

Ⅱ. In 1992, the US closed down its last military bases on the islands. Today, the Muslims, and some of the isolated tribes, are the only people whose culture remains unadulterated by Spanish and American influences.

The Philippines are chiefly of volcanic origin. Most of the larger islands are traversed by mountain ranges. Narrow coastal plains, wide valleys, volcanoes, dense forests, and mineral and hot springs further characterize the larger islands. Its total land area of almost 300,000 square kilometers includes mountain ranges, fertile coastal and central plains, rolling uplands and a coastline of 18,411 kilometers of which there are 60 natural harbors.

Its climate is generally tropical, with distinct seasons: the rainy season from June to September, cool and dry from October to February, and hot and mainly dry from March to May. Evenings are cooler. Typhoons occasionally occur from June to September. Average temperatures range from 24℃ to 31℃. The best time to visit is from November to March, when temperatures are cool and pleasant. April and May are very hot and humid. Avoid the rainy season from June to September, as roads are often damaged by flooding.

The great majority of the people of the Philippines belong to the Malay group and are known as Filipinos. Other groups include the Negritos (negroid pygmies) and the Dumagats (similar to the Papuans of New Guinea), and there is a small Chinese minority. The Filipinos constitute one of the largest Christian group in Asia. Roman Catholicism is professed by over 80% of the population and the rest are Protestants, the Philippine Independent Church.

The geography and history of the Philippines have conspired to produce a multiplicity of languages, some 80 dialects in total. The official national language is Pilipino. A considerable number of Filipinos speak English, the nation's second language. English is generally used for educational, governmental and commercial purposes and is widely understood since it is the medium of instruction in schools. The Philippines are the third largest group of English speaking people in the world, after the United States and the United Kingdom.

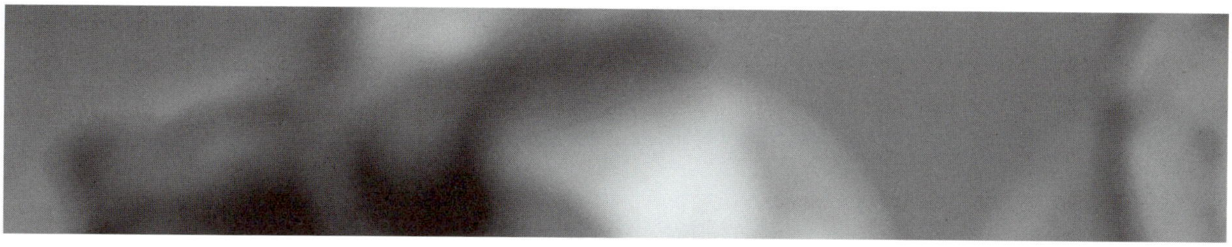

Philippines

CHAPTER 6

Shopping & Dining in the Philippines

Unit 2

Vocabulary & Grammar Practice

[1] Which of the following is closest to the meaning of the underlined word?

World-famous Philippine furniture made from bamboo or exquisitely carved wood can be priceless.

a) cheap
b) trivial
c) resonable
d) very valuable

[2] Which of the following best completes the sentences?

The most obvious Chinese contribution is noodles, (   ) form the basis of the popular dishes.

a) that
b) who
c) what
d) which

[3] Match each word in the first column with its meaning in the second column.

a) statue •	• a) figure of a person, animal, etc. in wood, stone, bronze, etc.
b) icon •	• b) material formed by weaving or knitting natural or synthetic fibers
c) cloth •	• c) an idol
d) fiber •	• d) invaluable
e) priceless •	• e) a natural or synthetic filament, as of cotton or nylon
f) virtually •	• f) to explain
g) account for •	• g) to take the skin off
h) marinate •	• h) to soak (meat, for example) in a marinade
i) peel •	• i) cheap
j) inexpensive •	• j) in fact, nearly

Reading or Listening Practice

[1] Think about the following questions.

1. *List products that can be purchased in the Philippines.*

2. *Name foods you can enjoy in the Philippines.*

3. *Write the key points, based on what you heard (read) from the below passages.*

[2] Read or listen to the following passages and answer the above questions.

Philippine products include handicraft items such as carved statues and religious icons; household items such as the Tiffany lamps; jewelry made from gold, silver, brass and pearl; baskets, jars, vases. They include ready-to-wear dresses in the most modern fashions as well as knit wear and traditional clothes, the national costume made of cloth woven from banana fiber or pineapple fiber. World-famous Philippine furniture made from bamboo rattan or exquisitely carved wood can be priceless. Other items include snake or crocodile skin leather products, antiques and shell product. Virtually everything in the Philippines can be bought in Metro Manila. Just along the Tourist Belt, a tourist can acquire a wide variety of items from rows of specialty shops.

Like the culture in general, Filipino food is basically of Malay origin, with Spanish, Chinese, and American influences. Some standard dishes, such as the coconut-based ginattan, have retained their Malay origin. The most obvious Chinese contribution is noodles, which form the basis of the popular dishes. Regardless of origin, lechon lumpia, and pork adobo are now considered national dishes. Regional variations in the fresh ingredients available account for provincial specialties. Among local specialties are lechon (suckling pig roasted over a charcoal pit and served with pork-liver sauce), adobo (marinated pork and chicken stew), kare-kare (chicken innards marinated in hot soup and stewed in peanut butter) and sinigang (a delicious sour soup). Tropical fruits are also delicious. During summer, try out halo-halo, a milkshake filled with fruit slices. San Miguel beer is both good and inexpensive.

CHAPTER 6

Philippines

Language Practice | Unit 3

How do you say the following in English?

1. 필리핀은 아시아태평양에 자리하고 있는 군도이다.

2. 더 북쪽에는 일본이 있다.

3. 서쪽에 싱가포르, 말레이시아, 태국이 놓여있다.

4. 대나무로 만들어진 필리핀 가구는 값을 매길 수 없을 정도로 값지다.

5. Cebu는 Manila에서 비행기로 약 한 시간 거리에 있다.

Incomplete Sentences

Choose the word and phrase that best completes the sentence.

1. *The company will provide premium services __________ all aspects of people's lives.*

a) which covers b) which cover
c) which is cover d) which is covering

2. *Park was a part of a team __________ investigated police officers.*

a) whom b) that
c) which d) whose

3. *The job opportunities __________ offered to foreign students are not enough.*

a) who is b) which is
c) whom d) which are

4. *A friend __________ I can have good conversations with is important to me.*

a) whose b) which
c) who d) whom

5. *The investigation is based on a petition __________ by conservative activists last month.*

a) filed b) filing
c) which filed d) which is filing

6. *__________ who wish to attend the session are required to visit our website.*

a) These b) That
c) Those d) This

7. *The Seoul Metropolitan Government will create a new tourism slogan for the capital, __________ will replace the current "Hi Seoul."*

a) that b) which
c) whose d) and

8. *Mr. Lee denied allegations __________ he used his influence.*

a) which
b) in which
c) whom
d) that

9. *People __________ infected with MERS have a high fever, coughing, and respiratory distress.*

a) who are
b) which are
c) that is
d) whom

10. *The book __________ I bought for my sister was interesting.*

a) that
b) whose
c) whom
d) who

11. *A police search dog discovered his body __________ from a tree.*

a) was hanging
b) hanging
c) that was hung
d) that hung

12. *The theater has enjoyed a renaissance with a wide range of performances, many tickets of __________ sold out in minutes.*

a) them
b) which
c) it
c) that

13. *It is difficult to determine __________ claims are true.*

a) that
b) which
c) whose
d) whom

14. *I know that man __________ I met yesterday at the book store.*

a) who
b) which
c) whom
d) whose

Incomplete Texts

Choose the best word or phrase for each blank.

Questions 1 through 3 refer to the following story.

HALLOWEEN

Candy, fireworks, costumes. Halloween has it all. Halloween ______________ is celebrated

1. a) who
   b) which
   c) whose
   d) whom

on Oct. 31st is a time for children to decorate their classrooms. They beautify them with scary pictures of jack-o-lanterns, _______ are a symbol of Halloween.

2. a) that
   b) who
   c) whose
   d) which

At home, they prepare for the big night. Children, teenagers, and some university students who dress up in costumes go from house to house.
They shout "trick or treat" and are given candy, which they usually put in a bag or empty pillow case.
This custom originated as a Celtic festival in Britain several hundred years ago. It was originally called Samhain, _________ was the last day of summer(Oct. 31st).

3. a) that
   b) what
   c) which
   d) who

People lit big fires and dressed in scary costumes to frighten off evil spirits.
They believed that ghosts came out of their graves on the evening of Oct. 31st. That is how the festival gained the name, Halloween, meaning "All Hallow's Eve."

Questions 4 through 6 refer to the following news article.

Northern Europe Popular for Young Koreans

Northern European countries are becoming more popular migration destinations for young Koreans. Foreign ministry data shows the number of Koreans ________ in Denmark and

4. a) who lives
   b) who are living
   c) who live
   d) who lived

Norway has sharply increased from 767 in 2009 to 1,148 in 2013. Northern Europe has become increasingly popular after Korea signed a working holiday pact with Denmark in 2010 and Sweden in 2011, ______________ people under 30 to live and work in

5. a) that allows
   b) that is allowed
   c) which is allowed
   d) which allows

the countries for a year. Before the pact was signed, young people moved to Australia, Canada or New Zealand where anyone was eligible for working holiday visa. But the countries have become less appealing because of safety issues. Last week, a Korean man _________ in Sydney was found dead five days after he went missing.

6. a) who was stayed
   b) that stayed
   c) who stays
   d) that was stayed

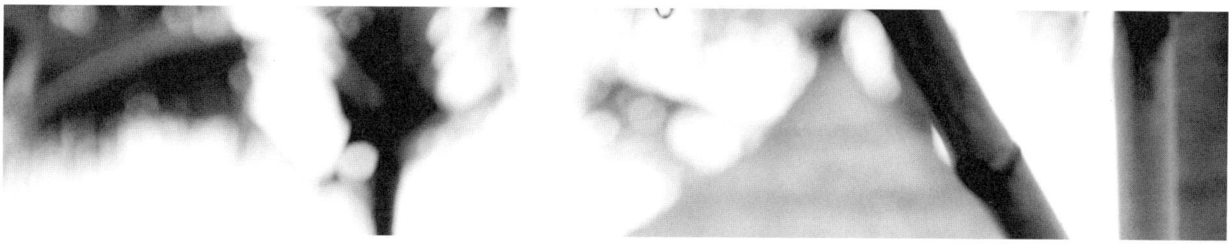

Answer Key

CHAPTER 1 China

Unit 1 Vocabulary & Grammar Practice

[1] b)

[2] a) farthest south

b) of race

c) of a different kind

d) number of people living in a particular area

e) an official process of counting a country's population

f) connected with beauty

g) large enough in amount or number to be noticeable

h) land or district

i) position of the rivers, roads, buildings, etc.

j) free from extremes

Unit 2 Vocabulary & Grammar Practice

[1] b)

[2] b)

[3] a) – a) b) – c) c) – f) d) – h) e) – d) f) – e) g) – g) h) – i) i) – b) j) – j)

Unit 3 How can you say the following in English?

1. Shanghai, which is located on the east coast of China, is the most populous city in China.
2. The Forbidden City, which was the imperial palace during the Ming and Qing dynasties, is the largest palace in the world.
3. The Great Wall, which is considered one of the greatest wonders in the world, was enlisted in the World Heritage by UNESCO in 1987.
4. The Summer Palace, which is the best preserved royal garden, used to be a summer residence of Qing dynasty emperors.
5. It is said that Chinese eat everything that flies except planes, everything on the ground except cars, and everything in water except boats.

Incomplete Sentences

1. A 2. D 3. B 4. C 5. C 6. A 7. C

8. B 9. C 10. D 11. C 12. B 13. A 14. A

Incomplete Texts

1. B 2. C 3. C 4. B 5. D 6. B

CHAPTER 2 Thailand

Unit 1 Vocabulary & Grammar Practice

[1] c)

[2] a) incapable of producing

b) of a countryside

c) of a town or city

d) able to produce good crops

e) something that is made to look like the original one

f) a type of pottery having a pale green glaze

g) a style of cooking

h) someone who sells things

i) a beautiful stone that has been cut into a special shape

j) extremely dry

Unit 2 Vocabulary & Grammar Practice

[1] a)

[2] a)

[3] a) – a) b) – b) c) – j) d) – d) e) – c) f) – h) g) – g) h) – f) i) – i) j) – e)

Unit 3 How can you say the following in English?

1. Thailand, known as Siam, is located at the center of South East Asia.
2. Established as a capital of Thailand, Bangkok is the heart of the country, geographically and economically.
3. Pattaya, one of Thailand's biggest tourist destinations, is an ideal place for water sports.
4. Phuket, the largest island in Thailand, is a very attractive island for sightseeing.
5. A theme park, Mini Siam, has scale models of Thailand' historical sites and temples.

Incomplete Sentences

1. A 2. B 3. A 4. B 5. D 6. A 7. B
8. D 9. A 10. D 11. C 12. A 13. D 14. B

Incomplete Texts

1. D 2. A 3. B 4. C 5. B 6. D

CHAPTER 3 Malaysia

Unit 1 Vocabulary & Grammar Practice

[1] a)

[2] a) the end of something
  b) a narrow passage of water that links two seas
  c) join together to form one thing
  d) place where two roads meet
  e) to cut wood or stone into a shape
  f) to make a hole through a piece of food
  g) a drink made by mixing different things
  h) a small shop with an open front
  i) the flesh of lamb or sheep
  j) a tool with a particular use in cooking

Unit 2 Vocabulary & Grammar Practice

[1] a)

[2] a)

[3] a) – d) b) – c) c) – e) d) – f) e) – j) f) – b) g) – i) h) – a) i) – h) j) – g)

Unit 3 How can you say the following in English?

1. Malaysia, located in the heart of Southeast Asia, is a multicultural society.
2. Johor Bahru, located at the southern tip of Malaysia, is connected to Singapore by a causeway.
3. Penang known as the Pearl of the Orient is a tropical island resort.
4. The historical building in Malacca were built by the Dutch.
5. Chinese comprise about a third of the population.

Incomplete Sentences

1. D 2. A 3. B 4. D 5. A 6. D 7. B
8. C 9. A 10. D 11. B 12. A 13. C 14. D

Incomplete Texts

1. B 2. D 3. A 4. C 5. D 6. A

CHAPTER 4 Singapore

Unit 1 Vocabulary & Grammar Practice

[1] b)

[2] a) to move away or back
  b) free in action and behavior
  c) an object kept as a reminder of an event, trip, place, etc.
  d) an object produced or shaped by human beings
  e) small object that is valuable because it is old, beautiful, or rare
  f) an area away from the center of a town or city, where a lot of people live
  g) a store that sells the goods of a particular manufacturer or wholesaler
  h) someone who sells things in a shop
  i) offer made in reply to an offer made by somebody else
  j) having a pleasant smell

Unit 2 Vocabulary & Grammar Practice

[1] a)

[2] b)

[3] a) – f) b) – d) c) – a) d) – b) e) – h) f) – j) g) – c) h) – g) i) – e) j) – i)

Unit 3 How can you say the following in English?

1. It is common for people to use 4 languages in Singapore.
2. Clarke Quay is Singapore's only riverside village combining dining, shopping, and entertainment.
3. Sentosa Island is Singapore's mega theme-park, attracting numerous visitors every year.
4. Underwater World has been praised as Asia's most exciting tropical ocenarium.
5. Praised as Asia's most exciting tropical oceanarium, Under World has a 80-meter transparent tunnel.

Incomplete Sentences

1. C 2. D 3. D 4. A 5. D 6. B 7. D
8. D 9. D 10. A 11. C 12. A 13. D 14. A

Incomplete Texts

1. C 2. A 3. B 4. D 5. A 6. C

CHAPTER 5 Indonesia

Unit 1 Vocabulary & Grammar Practice

[1] c)

[2] a) a sharply pointed mountain top
  b) treated animal skin used for making shoes, bags, etc.
  c) group of many islands
  d) to surround on all sides
  e) a wide view of country scenery
  f) to move from one place to another
  g) a building in which Muslims worship
  h) a large piece of land where crops are grown.
  i) the heavy rains which fall in India and neighboring countries
  j) to prevent from acting

Unit 2 Vocabulary & Grammar Practice

[1] a)

[2] c)

[3] a) – a) b) – e) c) – b) d) – f) e) – g) f) – c) g) – j) h) – d) i) – i) j) – h)

Unit 3 How can you say the following in English?

1. Indonesia, the largest archipelago in the world, is the largest country in Southeast Asia.
2. Indonesia is situated around the equator.
3. The population of Indonesia is predominantly Muslims (Moslems).
4. Chinese restaurants are found all over the country in Indonesia.
5. Bali is based on Hinduism.

Incomplete Sentences

1. C 2. A 3. D 4. A 5. B 6. C 7. A
8. B 9. D 10. A 11. A 12. C 13. A 14. D

Incomplete Texts

1. B 2. C 3. A 4. C 5. A 6. B

CHAPTER 6 Philippines

Unit 1 Vocabulary & Grammar Practice

[1] d)

[2] a) a native or inhabitant of the Philippines
    b) the Filipino language
    c) fairly large in amount, size, or degree
    d) figure of a person, animal, etc. in wood, stone, bronze, etc.
    e) to take possession of a country
    f) to take the skin off
    g) to take the vows of a religious order
    h) material formed by weaving
    i) the act or action of teaching
    j) pass across

Unit 2 Vocabulary & Grammar Practice

[1] d)

[2] d)

[3] a) – a) b) – c) c) – b) d) – e) e) – d) f) – j) g) – f) h) – h) i) – g) j) – i)

Unit 3 How can you say the following in English?

1. The Philippines is an archipelago situated in the Asia Pacific.
2. Further north is Japan.
3. To the west lies Singapore, Malaysia, and Thailand.
4. Philippine furniture made from bamboo are priceless.
5. Cebu is about an hour flight from Manila.

Incomplete Sentences

1. B 2. B 3. D 4. D 5. A 6. C 7. B
8. D 9. A 10. A 11. B 12. B 13. C 14. C

Incomplete Texts

1. B 2. D 3. C 4. B 5. D 6. B

REFERENCES

Byram, M.(1997). *Teaching and assessing intercultural communicative competence.* Clevedon, UK: Multilingual Matters.

Chang, H-j.(2012). Empowering intercultural communicative competence through metacognitive reading strategy. *English Language & Literature Teaching, 18*(2), 1-20.

Chang, H-J., & Seong, M-H.(2016). *English and culture in tourism.* Seoul: Baeksan Publishing Co.

Cheon, G. M., & Starosa, W. J.(2000). The development and validation of the intercultural sensitivity scale. *Human Communication, 3*, 1-15.

Hadley, A. O.(2001). *Teaching language in context.* Boston, MA: Heinle & Heinle.

Knop, C. K.(1976). On using culture capsules and culture assimilators, *The French Review, 50*(1), 54-64

Kramsch, C.(1993). *Context and culture in language teaching.* Oxford: Oxford University Press.

Kramsch, C.(2001). Intercultural communication in Carter, R., & Nunan, D.(Eds.), *Cambridge guide teaching English to speakers of other languages* (pp.201- 206). Cambridge: Cambridge University Press.

Lustig, M. W., & Koester, J.(1996). *Intercultural competence: Interpersonal communication across cultures.* New York: Harper Collins College Publishers.

Savignon, S. J.(1987). Communicative language teaching. *Teaching Foreign Language, 26*(4), 235-242.

Sercu, L.(2000). *Acquiring intercultural communicative competence from textbooks.* Belguium: Leuven University Press.

Seong, Myeong-Hee.(2004). *Practical Tourism English Reading.* Seoul: Baeksan Publishing Co.

Seong, Myeong-Hee.(2011). *Travel English.* Seoul: Baeksan Publishing Co.

Seong, Myeong-Hee.(2015). *English for tourism.* Seoul: Baeksan Publishing Co.

http://www.en.wikipedia.org

http://www.en.wikipedia.org/wiki/China

http://www.en.wikipedia.org/wiki/Thailand

http://www.en.wikipedia.org/wiki/Malaysia

http://www.en.wikipedia.org/wiki/Indonesia

http://www.en.wikipedia.org/wiki/Singapore

http://www.en.wikipedia.org/wiki/Philippines